Wisconsin Wildlife

Animals & Mammals

Billy Grinslott & Kinsey Marie Books

ISBN - 9781965098691

Chipmunks are found in many areas. Chipmunks are small members of the squirrel family. They like to eat nuts and seeds. Chipmunks are most active during the day, especially at dawn and dusk. They have pouches inside of their cheeks so they can carry food. They are very friendly and will take food from your hand. Chipmunks need about 15 hours of sleep per day. The smallest chipmunk species is Tamias minimus, which is found throughout North America.

There are many squirrels in the wild. You may see a red or gray squirrel. The most popular is the gray squirrel. Squirrels are very acrobatic and can climb trees. Their favorite food is acorns. Squirrels hide their food in many small stashes and can find more than 90% of them later. Squirrels are fast and can run up a tree at 12 miles per hour. Newborn squirrels are blind, deaf, and hairless, and rely on their mother until they mature.

Flying Squirrels don't fly like birds. They don't have wings. They have skin that is attached to their legs. When they jump from a tree, they spread their legs out and glide through the air. Most glides are 30 feet from tree to tree. But they can glide up to 150 feet.

There are many types of rabbits in the wild. The most common is the cottontail. Rabbits are cute, friendly, and fun to watch. Many people have rabbits for pets. They have soft fluffy fur. They are called cottontails because they have a white fluffy tail that looks like a cotton ball.

The hare is bigger than a rabbit with longer ears and legs. Their longs legs help them to run fast. They are agile and faster than most rabbits. Hares have excellent hearing and vision. Hares have large ears and eyes that are positioned on the sides of their head, giving them a wide field of vision. Hares can change color. Hares have the ability to change color depending on the season and their surroundings.

Pee-ewe what is that stinky critter with the big bushy tail. It smells bad. Skunks are normally curious and friendly unless you scare them. If you scare them, they will flip their bushy tale at you and spray you with a smelly potion and it stinks. Skunks spray a smelly, sulfur-based liquid from their anal glands as a defense mechanism. The spray can cause eye irritation and temporary blindness. Skunks are highly adaptable and can thrive in many different environments. Skunks have strong forefeet and long claws for digging. Skunks live in dens.

Porcupines have sharp quills to help protect them. A porcupine can have up to 30 thousand quills, they are sharp and will stick you if you touch them. Porcupines are excellent climbers with long claws. Porcupines are shy, nocturnal, and solitary animals that spend much of their time in trees. To communicate they make grunts and high-pitched noises. A group of porcupines is called a family.

Opossums or possums have strong tails and can hang from trees. One trick that a possum has, is when it feels danger is it will play dead. It will lay there and not move. Possums have white to gray face hair. Possums like to eat wood ticks. They are also immune to snakebites. Opossums are susceptible to frostbite because their hands and tails are not protected by fur. Opossums are marsupials, which means they have pouches for their young, like kangaroos and koalas.

Raccoons like to come out at night. Their eyes are made so they can see in the dark. Raccoons are highly intelligent and can solve problems. They can learn to open doors, trash cans, and other containers. They are called masked bandits because they like to raid and eat out of trash cans at night. Raccoons can survive in many environments.

Groundhogs or woodchucks are the largest member of the squirrel family. Groundhogs get their name because of their big bodies, and they live underground. Groundhogs are skilled climbers and swimmers. Groundhogs are true hibernators, sleeping for up to six months. Groundhog Day is where Punxsutawney Phil predicts how long winter will last.

Beavers use their teeth to cut and knock down trees. They build dams with them to block water, so they have a place to live and swim. They also eat wood. Beavers can stay underwater for about 8 minutes. Beavers slap their tails on the water to indicate danger. Beavers are the largest rodents in North America.

Otters have the thickest fur of any animal. The otter is one of the few mammals that use tools, like rocks to break thing open. A group of otters resting together is called a raft.

Otters primarily rely on their sense of touch, whiskers, and forepaws, in murky waters to locate food. Otters have built in pouches of loose skin under their forearms to stash extra food when diving.

Martens live in a variety of habitats, including forests, woodlands, and snowy areas. Martens can be distinguished from fishers, because martens are smaller, have orange on their throats and chests, and have pointier ears and snouts. Martens are part of the weasel family. They are very rare and hard to find. Their tail is long, about two thirds of their body size. There are 13 subspecies of American marten that are native to North America.

Gophers are little excavators. They have sharp claws and make tunnels and burrows underground. That's where they live most of the time. Gophers have fur-lined cheek pouches that they use to transport food. Gophers are active all year and are most often found underground. They rarely leave their dens, and when they do, they don't go far.

Badgers have elongated heads, small ears, and black and white faces. Badgers live underground with other family members. Badgers are very social and live in groups. A badger den or sett can be centuries old and are used by many generations of badgers. Badgers are very territorial, it's best not to bother them is you see one. A group of badgers is called a cete, though they are often called clans. Badgers are largely nocturnal but reduce their activity during periods of cold weather.

The American Mink lives across most of North America and is a cat sized. Mink are very skilled climbers and swimmers. They prefer to keep to themselves. They communicate using odors, visual signals, and other sounds. They purr when they're happy. Mink are agile swimmers, and they often dive to find food

Fishers live in the forests of Canada and the northern United States. They hiss and growl when upset. They are closely related to badgers, mink, and otters. Fisher young are known as kits. Fishers are one of the few animals that eat porcupines. Fishers are also called pekan, pequam, wejack, and woolang.

Mallard ducks are by far the most recognizable and popular ducks in the world. They live in just about every area of North America. Their estimated population is around 19 million birds. The male is easily recognizable from its white neck ring and green neck and head. The female Mallard has between five to 14 light green eggs. Most ducks don't have green eggs, so this makes them unique. The male Mallard is called a drake and the female a hen. Female Mallards quack. Males don't quack, instead they produce deeper, raspier one- and two-note calls. They can also make rattling sounds by rubbing their bills against their flight feathers.

Canada Geese are the most sought after and abundant goose in North America. They live in many places. Canada geese can travel 1,500 miles in a day if the weather permits. Canada geese migrate every year and if you are pursuing them, anywhere along their central flyway is great. The best places are Colorado, Kansas, Nebraska, Texas and the Dakotas.

The Midwest is usually regarded as the best place in the country to pursue ruffed grouse. Minnesota, Wisconsin, and Michigan have millions of acres of prime grouse habitat available, and much of it is publicly accessible.

Ringed Neck Pheasants are one of the most sought-after birds in North America. They are found throughout most of Northern America and Canada. Ring-necked pheasants are not native to the US. Instead, they were brought here from Asia in the 1880's. South Dakota is one of the best places to find Pheasants.

The Wild Turkey is a large, bird that is native to North America. It is the heaviest bird in the United States and can weigh up to 24 pounds. Only male turkey's gobble. Wild turkeys can fly. Wild turkeys sleep in trees. Their heads can change colors. You can tell a turkey's emotions by the color of their heads. Colors can change from red to blue to white, depending on how excited or calm they are. You can find wild turkeys in just about every state in America.

Loons are expert swimmers and divers. They have solid bones that make them less buoyant, which helps them dive. Loons have legs that are placed far back on their bodies, which makes them powerful swimmers but awkward on land. Loons have red eyes that help them see underwater and locate prey. Loons use their sharp teeth to catch fish underwater. They can swallow most of their prey underwater. Loons vocalize frequently with really cool wails, yodels, and tremolos.

Bald eagles are large birds, with females up to 43 inches long and weighing up to 13 pounds. Their wingspan can be up to 7 feet wide. Bald eagles build the largest nests of any bird, up to 13 feet wide and weighing more than half a ton. Bald eagles aren't actually bald. The name bald eagle comes from the old English word piebald bird, which meant white-headed bird. Bald eagles have the best eyesight of any bird. A bald eagle can see up to three miles away, which is about four to five times farther than a human. They can also see small details like an ant on the ground from great distances.

Weasels are the smallest members of the meat-eating animals. Although small, they do not hibernate and are active all winter. Weasels in northern ranges turn white in the winter to camouflage in the snow. Weasels have long whiskers like cats, to help them feel things. They even have long whiskers on their elbows. When a weasel gets annoyed, it stomps its feet, just like humans do. Weasels are quick, agile, and alert animals. They are excellent climbers and swimmers.

Bobcats are named for their short, bobbed tails with white tips. They have similar markings to lynxes but are much smaller. Bobcats live in a variety of habitats. Bobcats are skilled at leaping and can run up to 30 miles per hour.

The Lynx is larger than the bobcat and has lighter fur and more spots. The lynx is more than twice the size of a house cat. Lynx have natural snowshoes for feet because they have long hair on their feet. Lynx like to hunt at night. They have excellent hearing and eyesight, and can spot a mouse from 250 feet away. Lynx have colors that help them blend into their surroundings. Each lynx has a different pattern, similar to a human fingerprint.

Gray fox prefers to live in rocky canyons and ridges but can also be found in wooded areas and open fields. They have strong, hooked claws that enable them to climb trees. Which is abnormal for a dog species. Gray foxes are not observed as frequently as red foxes due to their reclusive nature and more nocturnal habits.

Red foxes have excellent hearing, allowing them to hear rodents digging underground from miles away. When afraid, red foxes grin or look like they are smiling. Red foxes front paws have five toes, while their hind feet only have four. Foxes dig underground dens where they raise their kits and hide from predators. A group of foxes is called a skulk or a leash. Babys are called kits and females are called vixens.

The coyote is bigger than a fox weighing between 20 and 45 pounds. Eastern coyotes are part wolf. Coyotes are great for pest control. They like to eat mice and rats. They can adapt and live almost anywhere, even in the city. Coyotes are very smart and have been observed learning and following traffic signals in some cities. They have a yip type of call when they communicate with each other. Coyotes are found in all the United States, except Hawaii.

Wolves, coyotes, and foxes are all part of the dog family. The timber wolf, also known as the gray wolf, is the largest wolf in North America. Wolves are legendary because of their spine-tingling howl, which they use to communicate. Each wolf has its own unique howl. Wolves are born deaf and blind, but their senses develop at about two weeks. They like to roam in packs of 2 to 25 wolves. Their territory size is 25 to 150 square miles. You can see gray and red wolves in many areas of North America.

The whitetail deer is the most popular deer in North America. Whitetail deer have good eyesight and hearing. They can detect small sounds from a quarter of a mile away. Only male deer grow antlers, which are shed each year. Whitetail deer are good swimmers and will use large streams and lakes to escape predators. A young deer is called a fawn, a male is a buck, and a female is called a doe. They are the most common deer species and live everywhere in North America.

Black bears are the smallest members of the bear family in North America. Black Bears love to eat sweet things like berries, fruits, and vegetables. They are good climbers and fast runners. They are excellent swimmers and can paddle at least a mile and a half in freshwater. They usually sleep for long periods of time and hibernate during the winter. They typically try to stay away from people unless they find food in the area.

Yes, moose are present in Wisconsin, although their population is small and they are considered a rare species, mostly found in the northern counties. Moose are built for cold areas and like living in cold regions with snow. Moose are the largest members of the deer family. Moose are huge and weigh up to 1500 pounds. Moose love water and are good swimmers. Moose have poor eyesight but compensate with a good sense of smell and hearing. At 5 days old they can outrun a person.

Yes, elk are present in Wisconsin, with two main herds: one in the Clam Lake area and another in the Black River area, Elk are the second largest members of the deer family. Bulls can weigh up to 1,100 lbs. They can run 40 miles per hour and outrun horses. Elk has a good sense of hearing and can swivel their ears back and forth. Elk have eyes on the sides of their heads and can see in every direction except directly in front or behind. They make a cool bugling sound when communicating with other elk. It's fun to listen to them.

Yes, there are feral pigs in Wisconsin, though the population is not considered a widespread or serious problem. Sightings have been reported in various counties over the years around Prairie du Chien and Gay Mills. Feral hogs are known for their high reproductive rates and their tendency to root up the ground, which can lead to habitat destruction. They are highly intelligent, social animals with a keen sense of smell and a surprisingly good memory. Wild pigs can be found in various habitats, including forests, grasslands, and agricultural areas.

Yes, there are bison in Wisconsin, with a significant number raised on farms and managed at the Sandhill Wildlife Area. Bison are the largest mammal in North America and weigh up to 2,000 pounds. Bison can run up to 35 miles per hour. They can jump 6 feet vertically and more than 7 feet horizontally. Bison calves are nicknamed red dogs, because of their orange-red color at birth.

Fun Fact about Wisconsin Animals

1 - The American badger is Wisconsin's official state animal, and the state is nicknamed the Badger State.

2 - Whitetail deer are known for their white-appearing tail, are abundant in Wisconsin, with males shedding their antlers each February.

3 - The black bear is the only species of bear in Wisconsin.

4 - If you exclude farm animals, the moose is the largest wild animal in Wisconsin, weighing up to 1,500 pounds.

5 - Coyotes are Wisconsin's most abundant large predator, and they usually prey on small mammals.

6 - Wisconsin hosts 668 native animals, including fishes, amphibians, reptiles, birds and mammals.

7 - The gray fox is the smallest canid (member of the dog family) found in Wisconsin. Gray foxes are casily identified by their gray coat.

Author Page

Billy Grinslott & Kinsey Marie Books

Copyright, All Rights Reserved

ISBN - 9781965098691

Thanks

www.ingramcontent.com/pod-product-compliance
Lightning Source LLC
Chambersburg PA
CBHW060852270326
41934CB00002B/108